More Christmas Cameos
a set of distinctive PIANO transcriptions • by John W. Schaum

❄ ❄ ❄ ❄ ❄ ❄ ❄ ❄ ❄ ❄

Index

❄ ❄ ❄ ❄ ❄ ❄ ❄ ❄ ❄ ❄

EXCLUSIVELY DISTRIBUTED BY

HAL•LEONARD® CORPORATION
7777 W. BLUEMOUND RD. P.O. BOX 13819 MILWAUKEE, WI 53213

ISBN-13: 978-1-936098-66-8

11-12

Up On the Housetop

Benjamin R. Hanby
Arr. by John W. Schaum

Allegretto

Toyland

from "BABES in TOYLAND"

Victor Herbert
Arr. by John W. Schaum

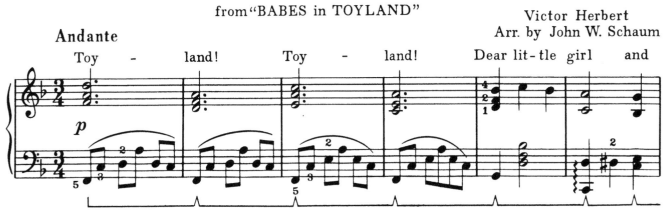

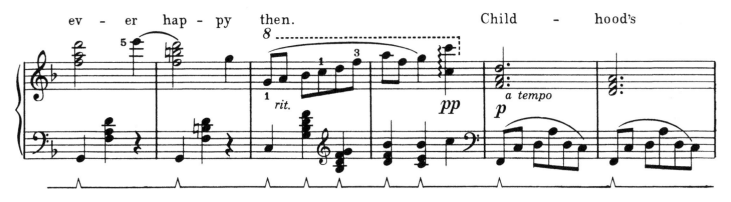

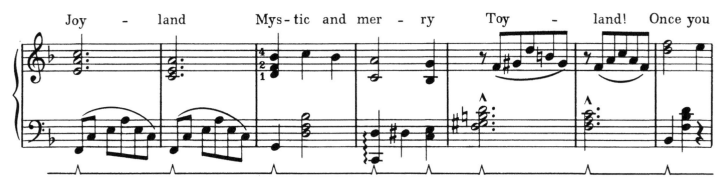

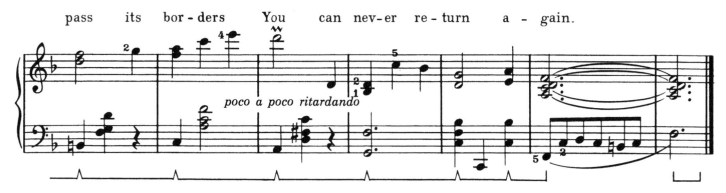

March of the Toys

from "BABES in TOYLAND"

Victor Herbert
Arr. by John W. Schaum

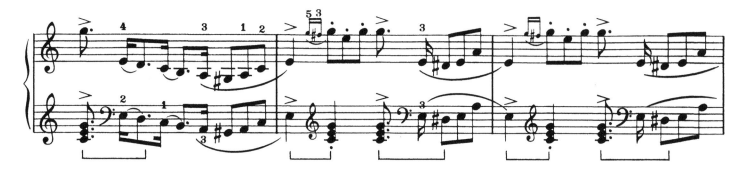

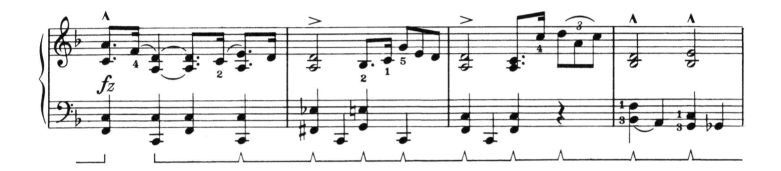

I Can't Do that Sum

from "BABES in TOYLAND"

Glen Mac Donough

Victor Herbert
Arr. by John W. Schaum

Moderato

Put down six and car - ry two, On the slate, On the slate,

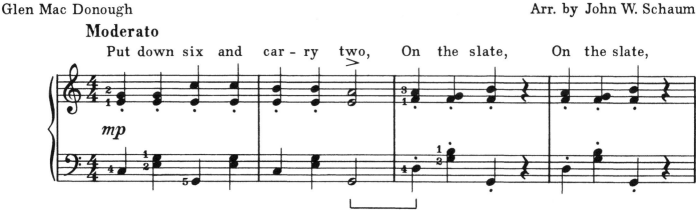

Gee! but this is hard to do; Scratch your pate. Scratch your pate.

You can think and think and think Till your brains are numb,

I don't care what teach - er says, I can't do that sum.

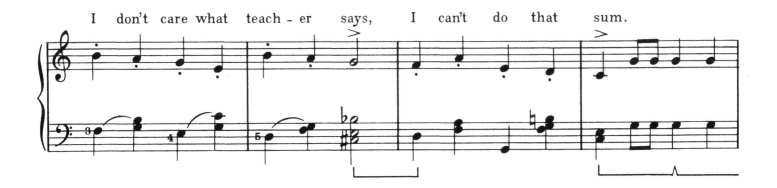

Variation

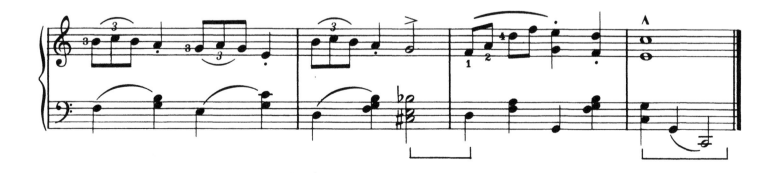

Deck the Hall with Boughs of Holly

Allegro

Traditional Welsh
Arr. by John W. Schaum

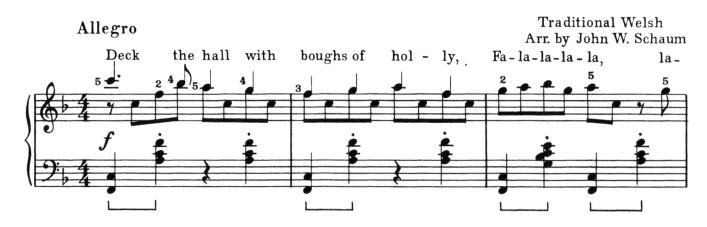

Deck the hall with boughs of hol - ly, Fa-la-la-la-la, la-

la - la-la, 'Tis the sea - son to be jol - ly,

Fa-la-la-la-la, la-la - la-la. Don we now our

gay ap-par-el Fa-la-la, la-la-la, la - la-la,

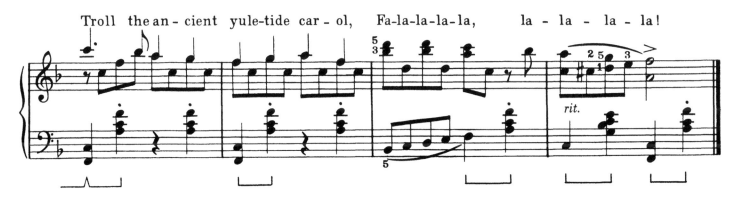

Troll the an-cient yule-tide car-ol, Fa-la-la-la-la, la-la-la-la!

rit.

Here We Come A-Caroling

Traditional English
Arr. by John W. Schaum

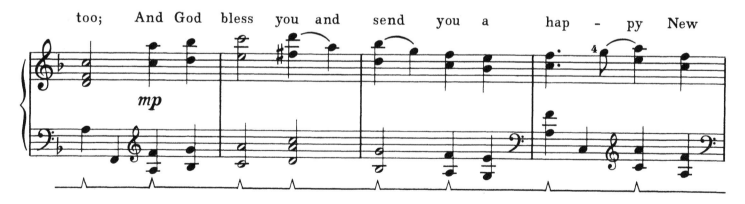

Bells Caroling

(UKRANIAN BELL CAROL)

Original Lyrics by
John W. Schaum

M. Leontovich
Arr. by John W. Schaum

Allegretto

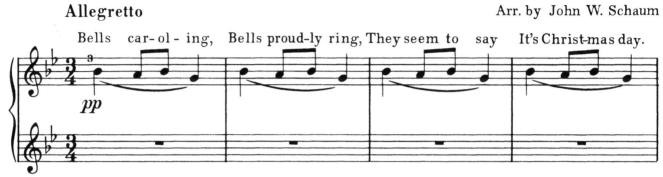

Bells har-mo-nize Sounds from the skies Bells clear and bright Ring with de-light

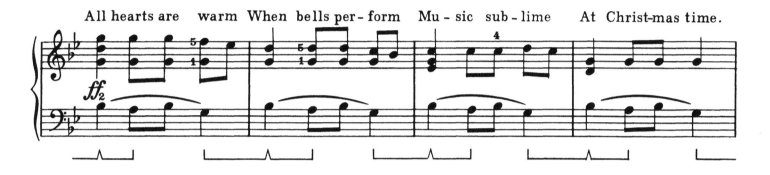

All hearts are warm When bells per-form Mu-sic sub-lime At Christ-mas time.

Wish-ing you a ver-y Mer-ry Christ-mas, Wish-ing you a ver-y Mer-ry Christ-mas

Bells rang the tone When the star shone Bells did pro-claim When Wise Men came

Bells ev-'ry where Fill-ing the air This is the morn When Christ was born Bells car-ol-ing! Bells!

We Wish You A Merry Christmas

Old English Carol
Arr. by John W. Schaum

Allegretto

Jolly Old St. Nicholas

Traditional
Arr. by John W. Schaum

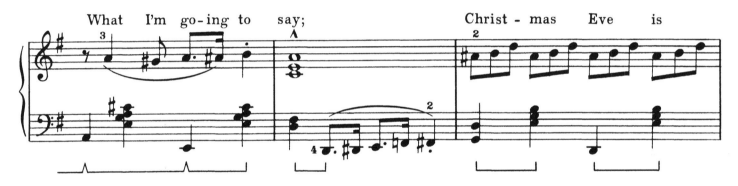

Jingle Bells

J. Pierpont
Arr. by John W. Schaum

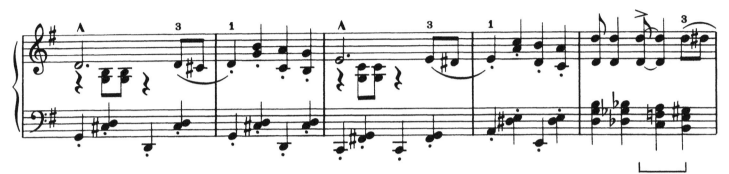

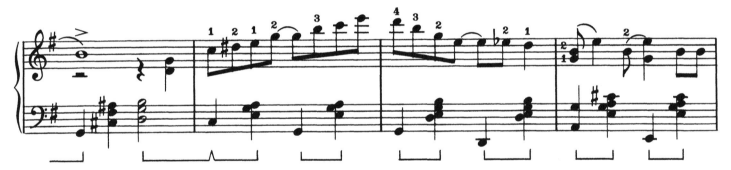

Go Tell It On the Mountain

Spiritual
Arr. by John W. Schaum

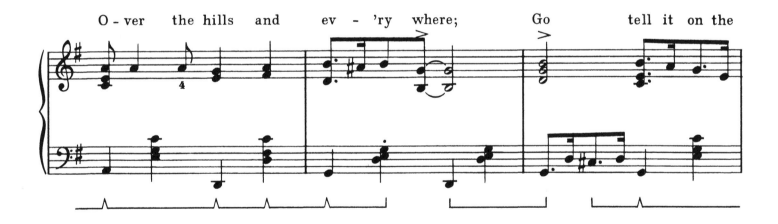

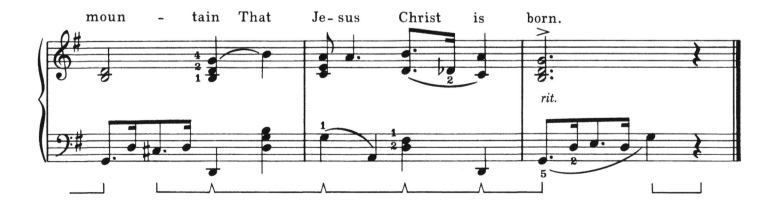

O Christmas Tree

(O TANNENBAUM)

German Folk Song
Arr. by John W. Schaum

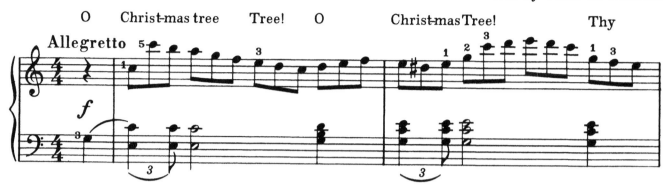

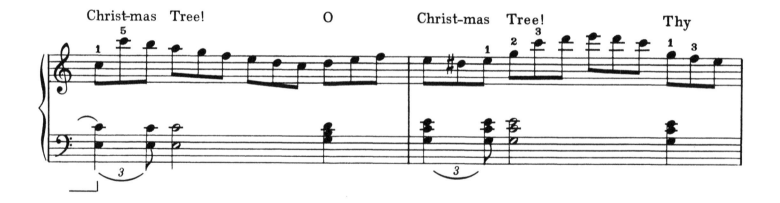

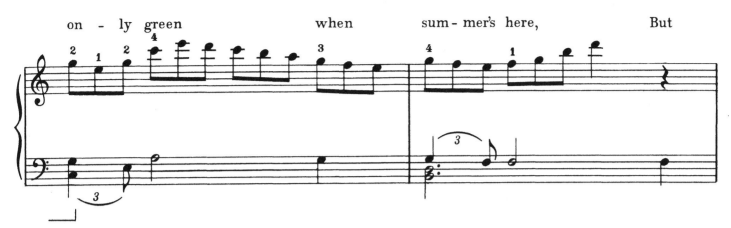

on - ly green   when   sum - mer's here,   But

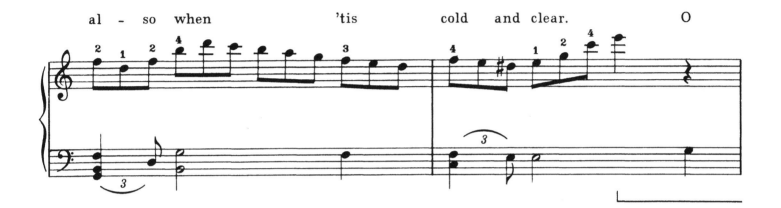

al - so when   'tis   cold and clear.   O

Christ-mas Tree!   O   Christ-mas Tree!   Thy

leaves are so   un - chang - ing!

O Come Little Children

C. von Schmidt

J. A. P. Schulz
Arr. by John W. Schaum

Allegretto

O come lit - tle chil - dren, O come one and

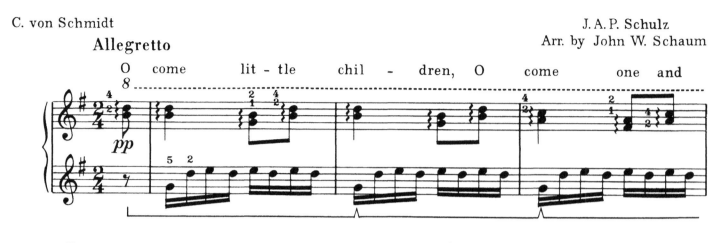

all. To Beth - le - hem haste, to the

man - ger so small. God's Son for a

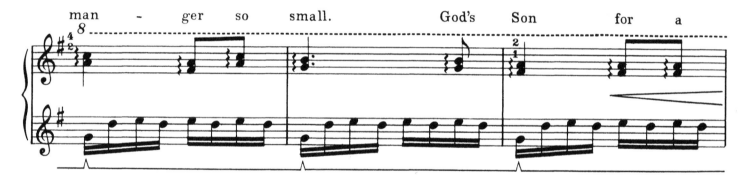

gift has been sent you this night. To

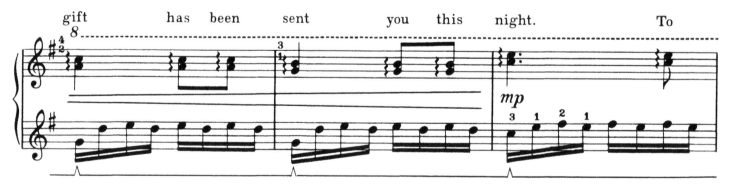

be your Re - deem - er, Your joy and de light.

Birthday of A King

W. H. Neidlinger
Arr. by John W. Schaum

Moderato

God Rest You Merry Gentlemen

Traditional English
Arr. by John W. Schaum

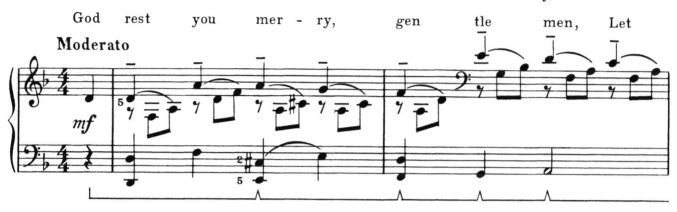

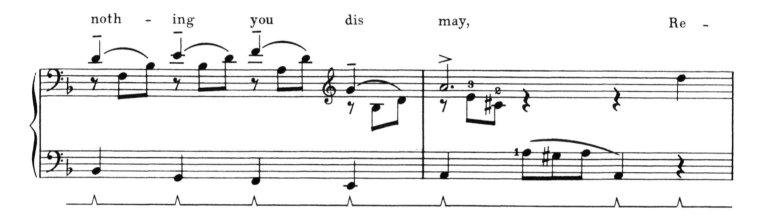

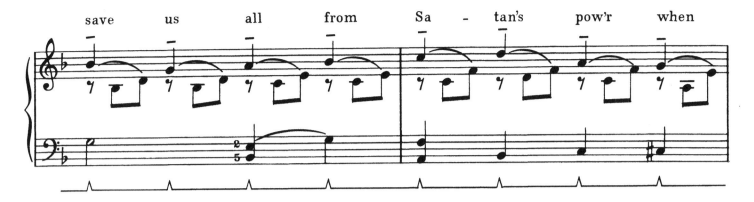

save us all from Sa - tan's pow'r when

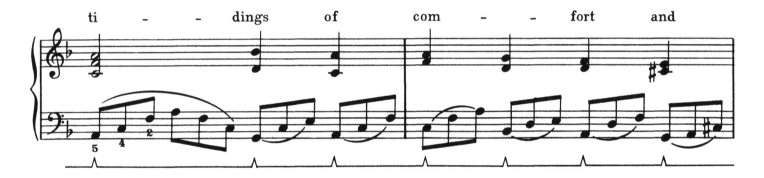

we were gone a - stray. O

ti - dings of com - - fort and

joy, Com - fort and joy, O

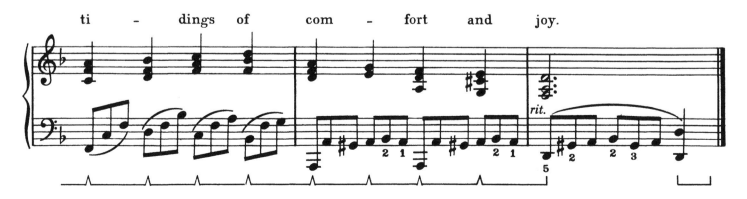

ti - dings of com - fort and joy.

You will also enjoy: Schaum's **CHRISTMAS CAMEOS** and **STILL MORE CHRISTMAS CAMEOS**